# Beauty of
# New England

# Beauty of
# New England

Text: Barbara Shangle
with contributions by
Paul M. Lewis and James Michael Fagan
Concept & Design: Robert D. Shangle

First Printing August, 1992
Published by LTA Publishing Company
Division of Renaissance Publishing Company, Inc.
318 East 7th St., Auburn, IN 46706

*"Learn about America in a beautiful way."*


This book features the photography of
James Blank
Shangle Photographics
Charlie Borland

**Library of Congress Cataloging-in-Publication Data**
Shangle, Barbara, 1939 —
    *Beauty of New England* / text, Barbara Shangle / concept and
design, Robert D. Shangle.
        p.      cm.
ISBN 1-55988-007-4; $19.95. — ISBN 1-55988-006-6 (pbk.); $9.95
    1. New England — Pictorial works. 2. New England —
Guidebooks. I. Shangle, Robert D.   II. Title.
F5.S53  1992
917.404'43 — dc20                                    92-27408
                                                        CIP

Copyright © 1992 by LTA Publishing Company
Division of Renaissance Publishing Company, Inc.
Printed in the United States of America

# Contents

# New England Photography Credits

*James Blank: Pages 17, 18, 20, 21, 22, 24, 25, 26, 27, 28, 29, 30, 31, 32, 33, 35, 36, 39, 40, 41, 42, 44, 45, 46, 47, 49, 50, 51, 52, 54, 55, 56, 57, 59, 60, 61, 62, 63, 64.*

*Shangle Photographics: Pages 19, 23, 32, 37, 38, 43, 48, 53, 58.*

# Introduction

Once upon a time there were explorers who discovered the New World and who laid claim to it for their respective countries. But was it that easy? Did the explorers, and the citizenry, and the New World in general live happily ever after? No, they did not. Conflicts and struggles for self identity, food, shelter, financial success, self government, independence, and whatever else is needed to go forward, were, and still are, the rule.

The "New England" region was first claimed by the French, then claimed by the British, and a see-saw situation prevailed. In 1497 an English explorer, John Cabot, who was actually an Italian named Giovanni Cabato, claimed the New World lands for England. In 1524 Giovanni da Verrazano claimed the area for his country, France. Of course the Native Americans were not consulted regarding their views on ownership, but they believed they had first-rights of ownership. In the early 1600s, Samuel de Champlain of France mapped out the Atlantic Coast shoreline, in particular current-day Maine, New Hampshire, and Massachusetts into Cape Cod. He was immediately followed by English Captain John Smith, who was employed by the North Virginia Company, an investment group interested in establishing settlements in the New World. Captain Smith gave the describing name of "New England" to this area.

The first colonial settlement was established by Samuel de Champlain at the St. Croix River, which is located at the upper most-northern edge of the U.S.-Canadian boundary on the Atlantic Ocean, at the time he was mapping the area in the early 1600s. Following close behind, a group of British colonists, representing England's Plymouth Group, arrived at present-day Phippsburg, Maine, in 1607 and established the Popham Colony. The Plymouth Company was a group of investors who were granted rights to the Province of Maine by England's King James I in 1606.

It was in 1620 that the English investment group known as the Council for New England was established. This group was created by the survivors of the Plymouth Branch of the Virginia Company. King James I gave the Council for New England the authority to issue land grants in the New World. The claimed area was bound by the Atlantic Ocean on the east, the Pacific Ocean on the west, and all land between the 40th and 48th north latitudes. For those not viewing a map, the 40th latitude cuts through lower New Jersey, westward across the bottom portion of Pennsylvania, the middle of Ohio, Indiana, Illinois, upper Missouri, separates Nebraska and Kansas, across through upper Colorado, Utah, Nevada, and Northern California. The U.S. and Canadian border from Washington State over to Minnesota follows the 48th north latitude, eastward. It continues above the Great Lakes, slicing through the Canadian Provinces of Ontario, Quebec and New Brunswick. England, indeed, had laid claim to a large portion of North America. The Council for New England was a charter group made up of survivors of the Plymouth Branch of the Virginia Company.

In the winter of 1620, the sailing ship *Mayflower* landed on Cape Cod, sending an investigating group to explore the land area of the Cape and the mainland, seeking a suitable landing site for the passengers. They made their selection and named the site Plymouth, for Plymouth, England. A group of some forty people, identified as Separatist, disembarked, looking ahead to a life of freedom to practice their religious beliefs. Separatists were known as disgruntled folk who broke away from the only accepted religious teaching in Great Britain, the Church of England. They were shunned, jailed, and generally persecuted in England. To avoid that type of treatment, they escaped to the New World. The Separatists, who considered themselves to be religious pilgrims, joined the other passengers and became integral participants in the Plymouth Colony.

More and more immigrants arrived. The struggle for Rights, the struggle for leadership, the struggle for development, land, and financial strength ensued. The Native Americans were feeling the threat. When ships first arrived delivering inquisitive newcomers to the lands, the Indians were interested in trading goods and were willing to establish friendships with travelers. It didn't take too long before the Indians realized that these travelers were increasing in numbers. They were settling in and establishing homes. The encroachment of their land was not well received.

The French were fleecing the areas for furs and fighting the British. The British were fighting the French, then the Indians. And for 150 years the famous French and Indian War played out. The British had a difficult task conquering "their" land. But they did succeed and in 1763 the Treaty of Paris was signed by the French, relinquishing all claims to the present-day Maine, New Hampshire, Vermont, Rhode Island, Massachusetts, and Connecticut, to England, as well as to most of the balance of the new country of North America.

The year 1842 was a critical year in Maine history and for the boundary designation between Canada and the United States. Up to that time, controversy existed between Canada's Quebec Province and the state of Maine regarding what was Canada and what was Maine/U.S. land. Quebec laid claim to land south, halfway between the 46th and 47th latitude, and Maine laid claim to the same region, continuing northward toward Quebec. The mother country, Great Britain, stepped in and claimed all the northern-most land.

Maine and the U.S. Congress were extremely serious about this boundary dispute. Maine gathered an army of 3,300 soldiers, the United States Congress pledged a 10-million dollar budget, and thousands of military troops were made ready to defend this country's position. Negotiations thwarted the war, known as the Aroostook War. The northern boundary was established on the St. Francis River, well above the 47th parallel.

The expression "Pilgrim's Progress" is exactly what made the country "go." The enthusiasm of the immigrants brought about the settlement of the Province of Maine, the severing of Maine from its owner, Massachusetts, and having the Province arrive to statehood in 1820, the nation's 23rd state.

The shoreline of New Hampshire, at Odiorne Point, is the site of one of the first permanent colonial settlements in present-day New Hampshire. David Thomson, a Scotsman, and a small group of followers established their settlement in 1623 at a town now known as Rye, but at the time, it was identified as Pannaway Plantation. At about the same time, brothers Edward and William Hilton arrived at a place they named Hilton Point, eight miles up the Piscataque River, known today as Dover. Even though the Plymouth Company issued the land grant to Thomson in 1620 and Hilton Point received its grant in 1821, the positioning of which town was really the *first* in New Hampshire is still under discussion.

This land known as New Hampshire was part of the land package controlled by the Council for New England. In 1622 the portion referred to as Maine and New Hampshire came under the control of two English merchants, John Mason and Sir Ferdinando Gorges. In 1629 the land was divided, and that portion owned by John Mason was named New Hampshire, in honor of the English county, Hampshire, Mason's homeland.

Development of New Hampshire was steady, but not strong. Residents were unable to develop stable, even leadership and controls. By 1641 the townships of New Hampshire placed themselves under the control of the Massachusetts Bay Colony, and there the control stayed until 1679. New Hampshire became a separate Province in 1679, due to a ruling by King Charles II.

New Hampshire has always been embroiled in political and constitutional activities. It was the first of the original thirteen states to adopt its own constitution. Town Meetings were and still are the rule. It was New Hampshire who gave the necessary vote to adopt the Constitution of the United States, establishing a two-thirds majority, and placing itself as the ninth state to join the Union. Currently, it is by state legislation that New Hampshire's Primary election day is always the first Tuesday before any other state's election day, firming its position as the first state in the Union to vote in the Presidential Election.

As the struggling New World residents were taking hold of their lives in the early 1700s, resentment of English control was growing. New Hampshire was pulling itself away from the English control and pulling itself away from the Massachusetts Bay Colony. It wasn't until 1740 that New Hampshire became an independent province, owning some 3,500 square miles and 28 townships.

The governor of New Hampshire, an avid supporter of the Crown, practiced land granting, mostly for personal gain. He claimed that New Hampshire's land extended west to include Lake Champlain. This land dispute was not settled until 1764, when the British Crown gave the territory to New York, establishing the western boundary of New Hampshire along the west bank of the Connecticut River.

There was a constant unrest among the area residents. It was during the 1770s the legend of the famous Green Mountain Boys and Ethan Allen came about. The local residents referred to the area as Vermont. And those folks were ready to fight for it. There was virtually a civil war fought to get the 'Yorkers out. And it wasn't until 1777 that independence was accomplished. For the next 14 years, Vermont acted as an independent republic. In 1791 Vermont was accepted by Congress as the 14th state.

The Connecticut River was the focal point of early immigrants. Adriaen Block, a Dutch explorer, was the first European to arrive in present-day Connecticut. He sailed from the mighty Atlantic waters into Long Island Sound and inland, up the Connecticut River as far north as present-day Hartford. The area was a haven for Dutch traders, who in 1633 established a colony at Hartford. In the same year, Englishman John Oldham, a member of the Massachusetts Bay Colony, explored the rich Connecticut Valley. He returned the following year, 1634, with a small group of adventuresome Massachusetts colonists, who, again, were seeking religious freedom. They established a small settlement known as Wethersfield.

Windsor, a small trading post along the Connecticut River was established in 1633 by William Holmes. He, too, was an English colonist from the Massachusetts Bay group.

Many of the Puritans of Massachusetts continued to seek religious freedom. It was through their perseverance that the present-day Congregational Church finds its roots.

For a common cause, Hartford, Wethersfield, and Windsor came together and created the Connecticut Colony, a religious colony. It was 1636. But a common bond was not enough to establish firm control of the land. More colonists penetrated the territory and established land claims. The New Haven Colony developed Quinnipiac, now known as New Haven, in 1638, followed by Milford, Guilford, Stamford, and Branford.

It wasn't long before the Pequot Indians realized that these newcomers weren't going to stay in one place; they were constantly acquiring new land — their land. The Pequots had to put a stop to this encroachment. Frequent battles occurred, fueling the fire for a major conflict. The Battle of Fairfield Swamp in 1637 saw Captain John Mason and his troops from Hartford, Wethersfield and Windsor annihilate their enemy, the Pequots. Mason told his followers that the enemy had been defeated and the victors were to inherit the land.

King Charles II granted a charter to the land called Connecticut in 1662, allowing virtual self government and freedom the other colonies did not enjoy. This went on until 1765, when England's Parliament passed the famous Stamp Act that placed a duty tax on many basic items used by the colonists. This, of course, affected Connecticut, as well as all other colonies in the New World. The citizenry rebelled. It took 16 years before England was defeated, but the patriots of Connecticut, alongside the patriots of all the other colonies, pooled their efforts and fought for the independence of this great country. That was in 1781.

Seven years later, on January 9, 1788, Connecticut signed the new Constitution and became the fifth state to join the Union.

Religious freedom, again, made people move. Move or run away from persecution. Move to unknown lands away from their new found homes in Massachusetts.

Roger Williams, in 1636, was the first settler into Rhode Island. Fleeing from the authorities of the Massachusetts Bay Colony, Williams was befriended by the local-area Indians, who were sympathetic to his cause. Land was given to him by the Indians for his settlement, which he named Providence.

The Bay Colony leaders found Roger Williams to be guilty of spreading heretical views — his own, personal views: Pay the indians for the land the English King gives away; government cannot control religious practices of its citizens; church members should not be the only people who can vote, but it should be a right of every person. (Obviously, he was ahead of his time.) He and several others, such as Anne Hutchinson, fled the ruling Massachusetts Puritan controls and established their own free homes in Rhode Island.

In 1647 the various Rhode Island settlement groups gathered together, facing England as a single society. In 1663 England's King Charles II granted a charter for the formalizing of the Province of Rhode Island. Fighting for total independence from England was their goal and their eventual achievement. Rhode Island ratified the Constitution of the United States in 1790, entering the Union as the 13th state.

# The Algonquians

The Indians of New England were of the Algonquian-speaking people, one of the largest Indian groups in North America. They spread themselves over a huge section of the country, namely the Midwest, along the mid-Atlantic Seaboard, throughout New York, the entire New England area, and further north into Canada. Though they spoke a common dialect, the Indians were self identifying by tribal groups, creating their own internal language and customs.

Connecticut, Massachusetts, and Rhode Island had the highest concentration of Indians, with the Mohegans and Pequots in Connecticut, the Narragansetts in Rhode Island, and the Wampanoags in Massachusetts. Historians claim that there were some 60,000 Indian residents in the area in the early 1600s. By 1670 that count had been reduced to 10,000.

There were several noted English-Indian battles during those establishing times. The Battle of Fairfield Swamp in 1637 saw the obliteration of the Pequot tribe. The English attacked with such vengeance that everyone was killed, including the women and children.

Many Massachusetts towns were destroyed during the battle named King Philip's War, which started in 1675 and lasted until 1678, two years after the death of the Indian leader, Chief Metacom of the Wampanoag tribe. The white settlers referred to Metacom as King Philip. He secretly organized the Wampanoag, Pocumtucs, Nipmucs, and Rhode Island's Narragansetts to rid their lands of the newcomers. This did not happen. The Indians eventually were defeated, but not before many lives of both fighting forces were lost.

Currently, there are nine reservations in the New England area. The identity of the proud Native American is making a resurgence. The Wampanoag Indians of Massachusetts, the Narragansetts of Rhode Island, and the Penobscots of Maine have organized to be identified as a viable force in this nation. They are, again, owners of "their" land. The courts of each state have negotiated with tribal leaders to settle disputes that began with the arrival of the first settlers in the early 1600s. Do not underestimate the power of the Indian.

— BJS

# Connecticut

Connecticut was present at the birth of this nation we call America. The heritage that activates the Connecticut Yankee is part pride in his state's crucial role at the start and part pride in Connecticut's continuing contributions to the physical, moral, and spiritual strengths of the United States. Connecticut today is a leader in manufacturing, advanced technologies, and service industries. Within its 5,000-square miles, outside of the big and little industrial communities, there is still plenty of wild and rural New England in the soft and lush Connecticut landscape. Only 100 miles west-to-east by 50 miles north-to-south, there are 253 miles of magnificent shoreline facing the Sound.

Several of the state's most populous cities have grown up from those early colonial coastal settlements, including Bridgeport and New Haven, two of the three biggest. Today the industrial city of Bridgeport at the mouth of the Pequonnock River is unusual among Connecticut communities in its lack of historical relics. Bridgeport, nonetheless, has been in place a long time, first settled in 1639, although known by other names until 1800, when it was incorporated as a borough. Its excellent harbor, once an active whaling port, now moves goods across the sea and people across the Long Island Sound. There is also an outstanding zoo and a couple of noteworthy museums. One is devoted to science and industry and the other to P.T. Barnum, the circus genius, impresario, and flamboyant entrepreneur.

Bridgeport is near the western end of the state's coastline. Even more so are Greenwich, Stamford, Norwalk, and Westport, cities converted by fast and convenient rail and road transportation into "bedroom towns" for New York City.

Stamford is a manufacturing center, whose residential section is built on hills. Stamford dates from 1642. Norwalk is the next big town east, an industrial center that was settled in 1649. A good sample of Connecticut's salt-water swimming beaches is close by in the Westport-Fairfield area.

The broadest bay on Connecticut's coast is the New Haven Harbor, 19 miles east of Bridgeport. Downtown New Haven is the stronghold of Yale University, founded in 1701 as Yale College at Branford. Yale moved to New Haven in 1716 and was given university status in 1887.

The long flowing Connecticut River makes its grand exit into the Sound some 30 miles further east of New Haven. Two venerable seafaring towns occupy opposite banks at this point. Old Saybrook and Old Lyme still have an early-days aura reminiscent of the time when "old" wasn't yet a part of their names. Many of Old Lyme's grand old houses were built by wealthy sea captains who sailed clipper ships along trade routes to the West Indies and Pacific ports and returned with fabulous cargoes. The town is a magnet for artists, famous and obscure, offering major art shows in the summer. Old Lyme itself is certainly an inspirational setting, with its handsome old houses, tall elm trees, and dignified white Congregational Church. The latter a favored subject of photographers and painters.

Old Saybrook is the fourth oldest town in the state, having been settled in 1635 by John Winthrop and a party from Boston. Saybrook Point was once occupied by the Dutch of Manhattan in 1623 but was relinquished to the English in 1633.

At the eastern end of the shoreline is New London, on the deep water harbor of the Thames River. New London is home to the U.S. Coast Guard Academy, and Groton, opposite across the Thames, produces nuclear submarines and puts them to sea at the Naval submarine base there. During the Revolution, New London and Groton skippers made a career out of piracy against British shipping and were highly sucessful in grabbing off rich cargoes. New London captains and entrepreneurs became wealthy on the whaling business.

Further east, just prior to Rhode Island, are Mystic and Stoningham. Mystic is on the Mystic River and Stoningham is nearby on a narrow, rocky peninsula that conveys a feeling of isolation. Both communities preserve artifacts of their 19th-century seafaring past, when whalers and fast clipper ships were prevalent.

New England's Connecticut Valley is where a lot of important things happen, and Connecticut's portion of it is no exception. The best farmland is in the Valley, so this is where most of the state's still-considerable agriculture is carried on. The majority of the inland industrial cities are here, too, either on the river or not far away. Government is one of the region's industries, represented by Hartford, the state capital and the biggest city in the whole valley.

Hartford still cherishes its 18th- and early 19th-century marine history. Marine insurance was the beginning of Hartford's many insurance giants, branching out to fire, accident, life, and other fields.

Beginning in 1635, Hartford now wears an old-new look. Right in the thick of things, downtown, is the historical Old State House, dated 1796. A few blocks away is modern Constitution Plaza, a raised mall with office buildings and shops; high rise office buildings for those business giants; the splendid Civic Center, full of modern business. Tucked in amongst all this are relics of the past, such as the Wadsworth Atheneum, the first public art museum in the nation. Under the umbrella of the Atheneum, several museums and library wings house the paintings of European masters and other art forms; historical collections such as early American furniture; firearms, rare books and manuscripts, and reference works. Located in West Hartford is the Mark Twain House, built by author Samuel Clemens, a 19-room Victorian mansion.

Wethersfield to the south describes itself as Connecticut's first permanent English settlement, basing that claim on the arrival of colonists from Watertown, Massachusetts, in 1634. It also boasts of possessing a number of the state's older dwellings, such as the Buttolph-Williams House built in 1692. The Michael Griswold House, known for its "salt box" architecture, was started in 1680. The Joseph Webb House (1752), the Silas Deane House (1766), and the Isaac Stevens House (1788) are a three-house museum complex.

A cluster of other industrial towns occupy valley sites not far from Hartford. Vernon, Manchester, and East Hartford are on the east side. New Britain, Bristol, Southington, and Meriden, the farthest south of these, is set among the Hanging Hills, considered to be some of the most scenic slopes in Connecticut. Beautiful little Merimere Reservoir lies alongside the rocky slopes.

Middletown is nine miles straight across the valley from Meriden and it was named for being midway between Hartford and Saybrook. It was settled by Hartford and Wethersfield Puritan Colonists in 1650. Wesleyan University, founded in 1831, is located here.

Between Middletown and the coast, one can travel through some of the most charming woods-and-hills country it is possible to visit. In keeping with their former calling, some of them, like Haddam, Deep River, and Essex, lure tourists with Connecticut River Cruises and excursions to Long Island points and beyond. Not far away at Hadlyme is Gillette Castle State Park, where stands a tremendous fieldstone castle built by actor William Gillette during the early years of this century. A little bit east of East Haddam, the little Eight-Mile River has carved a gorgeous gorge contained in an 860-acre preserve called Devil's Hopyard State Park. There's an extra dose of dramatics where the river drops over Chapman Falls from the rocks above.

North of Hartford is the widest part of the valley, a tobacco-growing region. Here on the rich bottomland, farmers cultivate high-quality, shade-grown tobacco, used for cigar wrappers. Windsor, biggest of the tobacco-growing villages, is a northern suburb of Hartford at the mouth of the Farmington River, and is one of the three oldest in Connecticut. Windsor has a great number of pre-Revolutionary houses. There is the Fyler House, begun as a one room dwelling in 1640; the Loomis Homestead, on the campus of Loomis School, a highly regarded prep school for boys; the Oliver Ellsworth Homestead, dated 1740.

Besides boasting of beautiful rolling terrain of the valley, Connecticut has some "high" points, too, the highest being Mt. Frissell, in Mt. Riga State Park, reaching 2,380 feet, located in the extreme northwest corner. This region is downhill country in the winter, a favorite of skiers.

The mountains feed countless streams, most of which find their way to the two principal rivers of western Connecticut, the Housatonic and the Naugatuck, which joins the Housatonic a few miles from the Sound. Many of the industrial cities are found in the Naugatuck Valley, such as Torrington, Thomaston, Waterbury, Seymour, Derby, and Shelton. This is home to the Litchfield Hills, believed by some to be the most beautiful place in Connecticut. The historic village of Litchfield rises nearly 1,000 feet up in the highlands. Birthplace to many famous people, it is the birthplace to the first law school in the nation.

The Housatonic Valley remains essentially rural despite the solid industrial presence of Danbury in the southern part. Southwest of Litchfield the valley is dotted with idyllic old villages. Just north of Danbury is man-made Candlewood Lake, stretching 15 miles.

Eastern Connecticut has long rolling hills and, until the arrival of paved roads, had very few persons living on them. Norwich, at the head of the Thames River, is the largest center of population. It may also take credit for producing the first steel nails in the nation. Just south is Montville, site of Connecticut's bloodiest Indian wars, fought between the Pequot Indians and white settlers over land possession.

Willimantic is 15 miles up the Shetucket River from Norwich, an industrial town and once known as "Thread City" for obvious reasons. The east-central part of the state, Willimantic excepted, is populated by a scattering of tiny villages hidden among the hills. Many of them date from long before Revolutionary times and with very few revisions might fit again into the Colonial time frame. One such village is Coventry, birthplace to Nathan Hale. And there's Storrs, home to the main campus of the University of Connecticut.

Centuries have rolled on since this land was first invaded by Indian tribes, then white settlers. The rocky points, sandy beaches, the rolling hills and valleys, and the islands off the shore have been somewhat altered since then by the villages, towns, and cities that have grown up. A great deal of its rugged beauty and antique charm is still present, waiting to be savored. It's a tribute to the Yankee genius for keeping traditions alive while adapting to the rapidly changing world.

— Paul M. Lewis

# Maine

Maine is the farthest eastern state. In area it is half of New England: 33,215 square miles. One of its apparently permanent features is the mystery it holds for many persons, even for some who live there.

Of course that marvelously tattered coastline comes first to mind when the subject is Maine. Bent and folded into countless bays, inlets, and coves, protected by granite headlands and ledges, and bordered by thousands of islands, it is a coast that is unknowable in its entirety within the lifetime of any one person. It is also a matter of austere old towns, where much architecture of the past survives. The look of coastal Maine is unpretentious, and so is the attitude of its people, part of the heritage that makes this eastward-pointing shore like no other.

Probably the world's most "bent-out-of-shape" coast is possessed by Maine. If you were a bird, you'd fly about 218 miles straight, but to drive every bay, inlet, and cape, the trip would take a while, because the distance would then be roughly 3,500 miles. The complications continue offshore with 2,000 islands, big, little, and in-between.

This is the Down East coast. Although nobody is 100 percent certain exactly where Down East is, Maine's coastline is considered by those entitled to have an opinion to be more Down East than any other part of the New England seashore. Quoddy Head is considered by some to be the "real" Down East. The fogs and tides for which the Maine coast is celebrated are the thickest and the greatest on these lonely eastern shores. True Down Easters take pride in having the world's foggiest fogs and tidal ranges of more than 30 feet.

The lower, western end of Maine's coastline extends 50 miles from Kittery to Cape Elizabeth, a fairly "straight" section. The southwest coast has many good beaches, with low, rolling countryside. The exception is Mount Agamenticus, a 673-foot hill that makes an impressive green coastal point of reference.

Some of Maine's best farmland is in this western coastal wedge. Rolling fields are edged with stone walls; dairy herds and their barns present a picture of substance and prosperity. The first Maine settlements were here, and this is still the most thickly settled part of the coast. Most of those early communities are still around.

Kittery is just across the Piscataqua River mouth from Portsmouth, New Hampshire, which makes it the entrance to Maine from the south. It stands in simple dignity facing the sea. Fort McClary is on the Point, where the settlers gathered for protection against Indian raids starting in the 1690s.

The Kennebunks, including Port, Beach, and Kennebunk itself, are half-

16

*Portland Head Lighthouse*

*Rural Vermont*

*Carrabassett River near Kingfield, Maine*

*Ashby, Massachusetts*

*Plymouth Rock Portico, Plymouth, Massachusetts*

*In the White Mountains, New Hampshire*

*Old Constitution House, Windsor, Vermont*

*Mystic Harbor, Connecticut*

*The Swift River, near Conway, New Hampshire*

*Mystic, Connecticut*

*Scituate, Rhode Island*

*Autumn in White Mountains, New Hampshire*

*Waits River, Vermont*

*Gloucester Harbor, Massachusetts*

*Rangely Lake, Maine*

*Second Beach, Middletown, Rhode Island*

*Rockport, Massachusetts*

*Bath, New Hampshire*

*Stonnington, Connecticut*

*Central Vermont*

*Acadia National Park, Maine*

*Ocean Drive, Newport, Rhode Island*

*Eaton Center, New Hampshire*

*East Orange, Vermont*

*New Harbor, Maine*

*Marlow, New Hampshire*

*Bass Harbor Head Lighthouse, Maine*

*Topsham, Vermont*

*Near Pittsfield, Massachusetts*

*Wychmere Harbor, Harwich Port, Massachusetts*

*Prescott Farm, Middletown, Rhode Island*

*Kent Falls State Park, Connecticut*

*Gloucester, Massachusetts*

*Minute Man statue, Lexington, Massachusetts*

*Little Lake Sunapee, New Hampshire*

*Gloucester Coastline, Massachusetts*

*Harkness Memorial Park, Connecticut*

*Windsor, Vermont*

*Bernard, Maine*

*Old Sturbridge Village, Massachusetts*

*Portsmouth, New Hampshire*

*Grand Island*

*Orrs Island, Maine*

*Jenny Grist Mill, Plymouth, Massachusetts*

*New Hope Dam, Hope, Rhode Island*

*Scituate Reservoir, Rhode Island*

*Grist Mill at Guildhall Vermont*

*Sunset at Menemsha, Martha's Vineyard, Massachusetts*

way along the western coast. They have reached a level of popularity as summer beach resorts that may tend to overshadow some of the places nearer Kittery. But there's another settlement on the way to the Kennebunks that also comes in threes — York Village, York Harbor, and York Beach — and is both old and attractive. Today York is noted for its abundance of memorable old houses and the presence of exemplary white-sand beaches in its sea-facing parts.

Biddeford and Saco, industrial twins, are two of the very oldest, and largest, towns here. They specialize in textiles and are located across the Saco River from each other just back of the coast. Just below Portland, by the crooked Nonesuch River, is Scarborough, settled in 1633.

Cape Elizabeth really put the cap on the western coast, as the differences are more noticeable than the similarities. Portland, Maine's biggest city, is just north of the Cape, on the western shore of wide Casco Bay. Portland is nearly an island in the bay, almost surrounded by its waters and those of Fore River. Casco Bay extends over some 200 square miles. The islands of the bay are called the Calendar Islands, they number 136, not 365 as the name would have us believe. Two big ones are Chebeague and Peak's Island, nearest Portland, the most populated. Exploring the bay and its shoreline will introduce you to a myriad of marine life, interesting harbors and sandy beaches, rocky headlands, and varied landscape. Several rivers enter the bay. Some old and important towns are situated around the bayshore and along the courses of these streams. One of them is Freeport, where Maine's statehood papers were signed in 1820. Brunswick is nearby and is the home for Bowdoin College. Brunswick to Bath is just a short trip on U.S. Highway 1. The town of Bath, where the Kennebec River comes out to sea, continues a long and famous shipbuilding tradition.

Maine's capital city, Augusta, is a child of the lower Kennebec, a river that is a major mover and shaker in the economic life of the state. Pulp and paper mills give Maine a big boost in the economic ladder.

Wiscasset, settled in 1730, was a prosperous coastal town, maintaining an air of Colonial charm with its wide streets, big shade trees, beautiful old homes built by affluent ships' masters.

On the sea edge of a ragged peninsula are the Boothbays, three towns along with Ocean Point clustered around Booth Bay. Bristol Peninsula forms the western arm of big Muscongus Bay, a wide, deep estuary furnished with a passel of islands. Pemaquid Point is a place much photographed for its scenic standoff between the evergreen forest and thunderous surf crashing onto granite ledges. The bay's eastern arm is formed by a 15-mile peninsula, with little islands scattered about.

Maine's biggest bay, Penobscot, outlet for Maine's biggest river, Penobscot, is 40 miles from sea to river mouth, and it's about the same distance across the Atlantic end. Big is also beautiful. Triangular Penobscot Bay is like a sapphire lake, studded with green jewels, its shores rising in softly rounded hills. State ferry routes from Rockland travel to some of the outer wooded islands, such as Isle au Haut, a large part of it located in Acadia National Park. Windjammer cruises originate in Camden and other points along the western shore. Camden and Belfast on the western shore and Castine on the eastern shore vie for the superior view of Penobscot Bay.

There is hardly a rival anywhere to the island that is at the eastern limits of the middle coast. Flanked on the west by Blue Hill Bay and on the east by Frenchman Bay, Mt. Desert Island is big, beautiful, and dramatic. Connected to the mainland by a bridge, Mt. Desert has a feeling of island-ness nourished by the wild grandeur of its mountains, forests, cliffs, lakes, bays, and beaches. Mt. Desert is the biggest of the coastal islands, 16 miles long by 12 wide, cut deeply in the middle by narrow, fjord-like Somes Sound. Bar Harbor is the peerless resort community.

East of Frenchman Bay the coast becomes something else again. All the way to Passamaquoddy Bay at the far-east corner, the shore turns more primitive. Towns are very scarce.

From Ellsworth the coast road passes high along the upper shoreline of deep-blue Frenchman Bay. The highway crosses the base of Gouldsboro Peninsula. East from Gouldsboro for some 50 miles is a group of tiny hamlets that make their way with fishing and lobstering, plus some sardine and blueberry packing. Milbridge, Jonesport, Machias, and East Machias are the bigger of the little communities, all of which have that strong appeal of places without pretense.

Here, where the east is as east as you get, is the realm of Washington County, the nation's early riser. State of Mainers who live here greet the day before anyone else in the United States. This is especially true for persons living in the Cobscook Bay communities of Eastport and Lubec. Then there's Passamaquoddy to the north and east, beyond Campbello and Deer islands. There's even more. New Brunswick appears on the north beyond Passamaquoddy, and eastward the enormous Bay of Fundy stretches to the shores of Nova Scotia, hazy in the distance.

Back of Maine's incomparable coastline is more incomparable country. The southwest and south-central regions are known as lake country, but lakes and ponds are spread all over the state, up into the northern counties, which rub borders with Quebec and New Brunswick, Canada. That long north-south dimension measures 405 road miles from Kittery at one end to Fort Kent at the other.

The western and southern lakes make up an exceptional vacation-land that is being discovered by a growing number of visitors attracted to these natural, unaltered settings. Cumberland County, which backs up the Casco Bay coast, has its own inland water network, Sebago Lake, Long Lake, and many smaller lakes, ponds, and streams. The gently rolling farm lands and forested ridges add another dimension to one of Maine's great and growing resort regions. The skiing is furnished by Pleasant Mountain, out of Bridgeton.

Oxford County, just north of Cumberland County, lays a long arm along the western border. The Androscoggin River comes over from New Hampshire and makes a tour of the County's mid-section before turning south toward Auburn and Lewiston,, next door on the east. Locke Mills, Bryant Pond, and Bethel are towns that do well by the recreational opportunities at hand.

South-central Maine is also lake country. The big industrial towns of Lewiston and Auburn, on the lower Androscoggin, are next to a region that runneth over with water. What dry land is found, rises in wooded hills and farmlands, especially along the Kennebec River. Augusta, Maine's capital, straddles the river in the midst of all this. The towns hereabouts have lakes in them, around them, and near them.

North-central Maine is represented by Piscataquis County and the northern parts of Penobscot and Somerset counties. Piscataquis County is home to Mt. Katahdin, highest peak in the state at 5,267 feet; Baxter State Park, 201,018 acres; and Moosehead Lake, 40 miles long and up to 20 miles wide. The Big Woods is located in the northern section, among forests of balsam fir and spruce, primarily. This is lumber country.

Most of the towns, farms, and roads are in the southern part of Piscataquis County, and the same can be said for Somerset and Penobscot, on either side of it. The Penobscot River cuts through the middle of the long county, passing through Bangor on its way to the big bay.

Another of Maine's prize treasures is the Allagash Wilderness Waterway that flows north from deep in Piscataquis County to the great arc of the St. John River around Maine's northern cap. Much of the waterway's flow is leisurely, but that changes when the Allagash River takes over. The river makes a splashy show in nine-mile long Chase Rapids before entering Umsakis Lake.

The western two-thirds of huge, Aroostook County are covered in thick forest and threaded by countless streams that make up the north-flowing St. John and Allagash river systems. The long eastern panhandle that reaches south to Mid-State is devoted mostly to potatoes and partly to people. The big towns of this northern domain are here and so are most of the smaller ones.

It seems incredible that the East Coast of the United States harbors wild country as fresh and primitive as this, relatively close to the great population concentration farther south.

— Paul M. Lewis

# Massachusetts

The South Shore and Southeast parts of Massachusetts make the "Bay State" nickname honest. The region is awash in bays, rivers, lakes, ponds, and history. Plymouth and Bristol counties share Buzzards Bay on the south. Cape Cod Bay forms a part of the South Shore, with lower Massachusetts Bay making up the rest of it. It is all a portion of the coastal lowland that spreads out from Rhode Island's Narragansett Bay on the southwest. Plymouth, home of the Pilgrims of the Plymouth Bay Colony, is still a comparatively small place on the edge of Kingston Bay. Plymouth has lots of competition in southeast Massachusetts. There is Miles Standish State Forest, a popular haven for campers; Cohasset and Hingham, two charming suburban retreats for many Bostonians.

The Southeast, all the way to the Rhode Island line, has six communities that are cities of moderate size. There is Quincy, just south of Boston Harbor on Quincy Bay, established in 1625; New Bedford, at one time the whaling capital of the world; Fall River, on the Taunton River where it empties into Mount Hope Bay. Taunton, settled in 1638, is 15 miles north of Fall River. Early in the 19th century, Taunton led in New England ship building. Dedham, south of Boston, lays claim to the Fairbanks House, believed to be the oldest standing wood frame house in the country, built in 1636, the same year the town was incorporated. Hull is another of those beach towns in such abundant supply on the South Shore. It is actually out into the sea just *off* the South Shore on the edge, crowded by Boston Harbor.

Cape Cod is linked to the very beginning of settlement in New England. Governor William Bradford of the Plymouth Colony was authorized in 1630 by the Crown to bring the Cape under his dominion. For a long time it had been home to several Indian tribes of the Algonquian nation. Various points on the Cape have figured prominently in the affairs of the Cape and the world. There are upper Cape and lower Cape towns, up Cape being toward the Plymouth coast and down Cape in the direction of Provincetown.

On Cape Cod and elsewhere in the Commonwealth, townships are sometimes quite extensive in area and rather thinly populated. For example Barnstable, the biggest town in area and population takes up 60 square miles, stretched over a landscape of interesting variety from Cape Cod Bay to Nantucket Sound, including some prize beaches on the Sound side. Barnstable Harbor is protected from the oceanic tides by a seven-mile-long beach called Sandy Neck. The south shore, or Nantucket Sound side, is where most of the action is, in terms of year-round residents. The town of Falmouth has its special retreat centers for its visitors. A quiet, historic town is Sandwich, which attracts tourists interested in the Cape's earlier days. Barnstable may be a bit more boisterous, although it has its quiet and attractive hamlets like Centerville, Cotuit, and Osterville. Hyannis is a trading and activity center, and attracts the "summer people" to its nearby beaches. Fleets of latter-day "clippers" are launched from the harbor waters of Hyannis Port. Yarmouth is next door to Barnstable, down Cape. It also enjoys both Bay and Sound environments.

The mid-Cape towns, around the Elbow, are interesting for a number of things. Dennis turns to cranberry culture and culture in the thespic sense. The Cape Playhouse in Dennis is the oldest, and certainly one of the most famous in the country. There is Brewster and Harwich, one north and one south. Brewster's history was forged by the exploits of its deepwater packet masters, who sailed to the Far East in search of trading goods. Harwich has lost some territory since the old days. Both Brewster and Orleans (past the elbow) used to be a part of it. But its cranberry bogs are still the champion producers on the Cape, where half of the nation's crop is grown.

The most far-out town on Cape Cod, in every sense, has to be Provincetown. The community is at the tag end of the long, curving sand spit. Few visitors know the names of every other Cape town, but everyone is familiar with Provincetown. Big whaling fleets were built in Provincetown, and with its magnificent harbor, it became the leading whaling port on the Cape in the 1800s, second only to Nantucket. Commercial fishing is currently very important to the town's residents. But today the fame of the place rests largely on its attraction for the summer people, who make up its "art colony."

The Cape Cod National Seashore now includes most of the lower Cape beaches from Eastham to Provincetown (about 35 miles). The long yellow, sandy shore is now a federal preserve, and a good thing, too, because its wild and lonely miles are no longer so wild and lonely. The Atlantic side of Cape Cod has become one of the most heavily used summer shores on the whole coast.

The Cape has an escort of islands south of it. Close by are the two big islands of Martha's Vineyard and Nantucket, both as famous around the country as Cape Cod itself. The 16 lesser known, mostly private Elizabeth islands, are across Vineyard Sound.

The villages of Martha's Vineyard resist over commercialization. The Victorian homes and buildings of Edgartown and Oak Bluffs reflect the great age of whaling. West Tisbury is another lovely old village. On the southeast tip, the sculptured cliffs of Gay Head display a brilliant range of colored clays. Martha's Vineyard is a magic place that still keeps its special aura in an age when finding something different is increasingly difficult to do.

Nantucket is an island, a county, and a town. For a while in the 1760s, it was the world's premier whaling port, until New Bedford took over the title. These days the 14-mile-long island, with its cobbled streets and grassy lanes, handsome homes, open moors, and ocean air, makes a living by luring crowds of visitors during the summer to discover the unique Nantucket experience.

It's really impossible to do justice to Boston in just a few words. Precious landmarks from the past have been given renewed importance as historic districts are restored and renovated. The Faneuil Hall market area is a happy example. The beautiful old Hall, classic Greek Revival Quincy Market, and the surrounding area, with its informal food stalls, is a real delight. Overlooking all this to the west is the Government Center, new Boston, along with a striking City Hall.

The oldest part of Boston is North End, crowded and colorful, home of two pre-Revolutionary shrines, Christ Church ("Old North") and Paul Revere's House.

Early 19th-century Boston is preserved on stately Beacon Hill. Famous Beacon Street borders "The Hill" on the south, running along old Boston Common and west through the Back Bay. There is Copley Square, one of the world's most beautiful.

Greater Boston has no peer among cities in number and quality of museums, libraries, and institutes of higher learning. Part of the Yankee heritage is the urge to improve the mind. The Commonwealth and Boston in particular devotes a lot of energy and resources to that end.

Two of the more famous places in the Boston area are Lexington and Concord. They share the Minuteman National Historic Park, which includes Concord's Old North Bridge, where was fired "the shot heard 'round the world."

The North Shore is hilly and rocky. The rugged coastline reaches out to Cape Ann, where the legendary fishing village, Gloucester, is found. Close by is Rockport, famous for its artist's colony.

The famous old town of Salem, the "witch city" is found on the southern curve. Besides having a Witch Museum, Salem has the distinction of housing architectural treasures.

Up north along the Merrimack River are three old industrial cities whose early prosperity was insured by the power of the river. Today Haverill, known for its shoes and leather goods, has the look of Old New England. Lawrence is a more typically New England industrial town. Once The Worsted Capital of the World, its textile industry is now more retired. Along with Lowell, the old "boss town" of New England manufacturers, both towns made drastic economic changes when the textile mills moved to the south, where labor was less expensive. Lawrence and Lowell have made a recovery for their people. Diversification was the answer.

All by itself, Worcester County is the middle of Massachusetts. To make it official, Worcester, the city, calls itself the center of New England. The hills, lakes, and woods of central Massachusetts help make Worcester and its surroundings most attractive. Other Worcester County towns are history-conscious, notably Sturbridge, Barre, Princeton, Lancaster, and Harvard.

The Connecticut River cuts a broad valley through the western side of Massachusetts, entering from Vermont on the north and flowing across the border into Connecticut. This is the Pioneer Valley region. It's a productive agricultural region as well as for education, being home to three famous colleges: Amherst, Smith, and Mt. Holyoke.

The weightiest city of the valley is Springfield. The city has achieved a name since post-Revolutionary days for its metal-goods industry, especially weaponry. The Springfield rifle is a famous example.

Pioneer Valley has its mountains, too, namely the Holyoke range, where you'll find winter skiing at Mt. Tom. The northern part of the valley has its mountains too. The town of Greenfield is found there, known for its Green River knives and being the eastern end of the Mohawk Trail.

The western end of Massachusetts is the least populated and exceptionally well endowed with natural beauty. The Berkshire Hills rise west of the Connecticut River and form the eastern wall of the Berkshire Valley. The Taconic Mountains hem in the valley on the west and house the high point of the state, Mt. Greylock at 3,491 feet. Not far is the Deerfield River Gorge that is famous for the blazing colors of its October foliage.

Way up in the northeast corner of the state, Williamstown lies in its own serene little valley. It competes with the other college towns of the country for the "most beautiful" title.

Pittsfield is the Berkshire County seat and its largest community. It is a thousand feet up in the rolling hills between forks of the big Housatonic River.

South of Pittsfield is the beautiful old resort town of Lenox, known in earlier times as a writers' colony. These days it is known best for Tanglewood, the summer home of the Boston Symphony Orchestra. Here the six-week-long Berkshire Music Festival pours out its elegant sounds to the mountains and forests.

Farther along on the Housatonic is the little town of Stockbridge, famous for the Berkshire Playhouse. Great Barrington, Egremont, and Sheffield are resort communities in the southwest corner, providing ski areas, period houses, and natural attraction. Close by is Bartholomew's Cobble at Ashley Falls, a wild rock garden with unusual plant species and visited by a great variety of birds.

— Paul M. Lewis

# New Hampshire

New Hampshire's story begins along the coastal plane between those two giants, Maine and Massachusetts.

Portsmouth, by many considered to be the first settlement in New Hampshire was first named Piscataqua, then Strawbery Banke. The name, Portsmouth, was adopted in 1653 when the town was incorporated. Strawbery Banke is now the oldest part of Portsmouth, the downtown section by the river.

Restoration efforts in Portsmouth have brought renewed life to much of the city. Historic places, landmarks and names have been rejuvenated, adding renewed interest and a new life to the area. As a popular resort town, Portsmouth has always excelled. But with the restoration of historic homes and the wharf district, it's even more attractive.

The other "first" town is Dover, situated ten miles inland on the Cocheco River. Two rather notable 18th- and 19th-century homes are gathered into the Woodman Institute, an establishment with historical and natural history collections.

The next two towns of historical order are Exeter (1638) and Hampton (1639). Exeter, beautiful and dignified, is the home of the illustrious preparatory school for boys, Phillip Exeter Academy. The 400-acre campus hosts elegant Georgian Colonial and Classical buildings.

Hampton, the fourth and smallest of the first four settlements, sits right out on the Atlantic, soaking in its history as a substantial harbor town of yesteryear. Like Rye and Wallis Sands, just north, Hampton is a well patronized coastal resort, offering wide, white-sand beaches.

The life strength of New Hampshire lies along the Merrimack River on both sides of the Merrimack Valley. The "big" ones are Concord, Manchester, Bedford, Merrimack and Nashua. Concord is the state capital.

Manchester is an old Yankee city that speaks several languages in addition to English. Immigrants flocked to the area from 1840 to 1930 to work in the world's largest cotton mill, the Amoskeag Mill: French-Canadians, Greeks and Poles. French is spoken almost as much as English is spoken. The mill is no longer operating, but the ethnic influence of its people is very much evident. The library and museum of the Manchester Historical Association preserves the history of the city and nearby towns in their collections and displays, going back to the Indian days.

The Merrimack Valley is indeed one of America's most historic places, as well as being one of the most beautiful. The landscapes are a scenic combination of hills and trees and streams, with here and there a charming old village. America's poet, Robert Frost, lived in Derry Village from 1900 to 1910, finding inspiration for many of his poems in this most livable place.

The lower southwest corner along the Connecticut River is a region of visual charm of old New England. Mt. Monadnack rises to a height of 3,165 feet overlooking the gentle up-and-down scenery of the Connecticut Valley. Found among the lakes, ponds, and meadows, are beautiful small villages, bursting with charm and history.

Keene is an industrial community, providing products from shoes to machine tools, toys, to textiles. Petersborough and Swanzy Center burst alive during the summer, providing music and drama revivals. The Cathedral of the Pines is located near Rindge and Jaffrey, a non-denominational outdoor shrine, honoring Americans killed in wars. Hanover may be considered the cultural center by many as well as being the home of Dartmouth College.

The Lakes Region of New Hampshire is generally considered in the east-central portion of the state, with historical Laconia being the largest town. Laconia was established in 1777. There are more than 100 lakes, with Winnipesaukee being the largest. The chief resort is Weirs Beach, receiving its name from the Indian's fishing weirs or nets used in the local waters.

The second largest lake is Squam, located at the north end of Lake Winnipesaukee. Extra charm and beauty were added to this lake setting, with dense forests and high green hills. The southern White Mountain peaks rise in the background. Visually, autumn is one of the most awesome times of the year around the lake, when the nippy New England weather turns the foliage into blazing splashes of color.

The White Mountain National Forest is 1,200 square miles of total beauty. Near where the White Mountains start are very appealing little resort villages, referred to as the Sandwiches. The Bearcamp River country is home to several mountain ranges reaching from 2,000 to 4,000 feet in altitude. The tallest of all is the Presidential Range, presiding at the heart of this mountain mass. Mt. Washington rises 6,288 feet, the highest of the ten presidential peaks, with the lowest measuring 3,896 feet.

There are nine notches (the same as gaps or passes in other parts of the country) in the White Mountain system. Pinkham Notch is on the east, Crawford Notch is on the southwest, and Franconia Notch is on the west. The primary roads through the White Mountain notches and valleys have been in place, in various forms, for a long time.

Dixville Notch is the farthest north of the White Mountain passes. Every four years the town of Dixville Notch is noted for providing the first presidential election results. Voters always cast the first votes in Presidential elections by entering the voting booth at the stroke of midnight of election day. The voting procedure is performed in the old Balsam Hotel Resort, the last of the great White Mountain resorts. National news agencies and reporters are in attendance to hear the announcement of the first presidential voting results.

— Paul M. Lewis

# Rhode Island

"Good things come in small packages," so it is spoken. And that expression can be appropriately applied to the state of Rhode Island. This beautiful little state, nicknamed the Ocean State, is nestled between Connecticut on the west and Massachusetts on the north and east. The mighty Atlantic Ocean, which provides the life blood for Rhode Island, pushes up from the south. Actually, that salty water penetrates north about 28 miles, up to Providence, by way of Narragansett Bay. Statistically speaking, Rhode Island is 37-miles wide at its widest point, west to east, and 48-miles long, north to south. Its shoreline is approximately 385 miles, traversing the entire water frontage, which includes all the bays and waterways of southern Rhode Island.

Viewing this state may appear at first as something that won't take long, because of its size. That's a *big* mistake, as Rhode Island has so much history, and so much going on NOW, that to fully appreciate what this free thinking, independent state has to offer will take some *real* time.

Going as far west as one can go in Rhode Island is a little watching resort village named Watch Hill, originally established as a lookout for pillaging British vessels invading Rhode Island waters. Today it's a quiet resort town spattered with beautiful Victorian houses and supported by tourists who gather for solitude and relaxation. Many small towns dot this area: Avondale, Dunns Corners, Misquamicut, Haversham, Weekapaug, and Quonochontaug, all supported by that larger town, Westerly, established in 1648 by newlyweds, John and Mary Babcock. There are plenty of fishing opportunities here as well as surfside recreations, available at Misquamicut State Beach. Winds buffet this southern coast, creating great ocean surfing.

U.S. Highway 1, part of the New England Heritage Trail, winds along the Atlantic shoreline, working its way northeast to Pawtucket, east of Providence, along Narragansett Bay. Many of Rhode Island's resort centers and historical attractions are located on or near this highway. Water recreation abounds, having big and little ponds available, such as Watchaug, Ninigret, School House, Pasquiset, Worden and Point Judith ponds. Public beaches and state parks along the way offer a variety of amenities, such as camping facilities, fishing, hiking trails, boating, and swimming areas.

Narragansett Indians, who were so helpful to the colonial settlers, made the area now known as Charlestown their tribal headquarters. Still observing their tribal customs and language, the Indian Long House is maintained, and it's still a center of activity.

Peering south out into the Atlantic Ocean, Block Island is visible some 20 miles from the mainland. First discovered in 1524 by Giovanni da Verrazano,

Block Island received its present name for the Dutch explorer Adriaen Block, who landed there in 1614. Today visitors use both car and passenger ferries available at Galilee on Point Judith, Providence, and Newport to reach this recreational rock, which occupies 11-square miles. Hiking and bicycling seem to be the primary mode of transportation on this tranquil island. The north shore is home to Settlers Rock, the site of the first settlement established in 1661.

Back on the mainland is the small town of Matunuck, just west of the fishing village of Galilee. Theater arts are practiced here, and have been since 1933 when Theatre-by-the-Sea was established. Many would-be actors and well-known theater artists performed here.

Narragansett Pier, once an exclusive resort town, sits quiety on the west side of Narragansett Bay. Both the bay and Pettaquamscutt River provide a full range of water sport activities for those so inclined. Manmade adventure is provided down State Road 108 at Adventureland, toward Judith Point. Fishermans Memorial State Park is located on this little finger of Land near Roger Wheeler Memorial Beach.

Northwest of Narragansett Pier, the historic town of Kingston sits among its many preserved structures, both 18th- and 19th-century homes and public buildings. A short distance is the memorial site of the Great Swamp Fight, where desperate colonials fought the Narragansett Indians for their very survival and for the continuation of settlements in Rhode Island.

Wickford was a mere English fort during the Great Swamp Fight. Established as a colony settlement in 1707, it became a key shipping port for agricultural goods from the area's wealthy plantations. Old Narragansett Church is one of the oldest Anglican churches in our country, built in Wickford in 1707 and relocated in 1800 to its present site on Church Lane. And there's St. Paul's House, built in 1847, found on Main Street. Smith's Castle is believed by many to be the only surviving building used by preacher Roger Williams. The birthplace of one of America's famous portrait artists, Gilbert Stuart, is near Wickford. Born in 1755, Stuart is noted for painting 124 portraits of George Washington.

Skirting U.S. Highway 1 is a "new" kid on the block, Quonset Point, established in 1941 by the U.S. Navy Department, which has a great influence on the goings-on in the Rhode Island area. For those familiar with the term Quonset Hut, this is where it was developed, that pre-fabricated metal building.

A few miles north is East Greenwich, one of those fast growing towns in the mid-1600s. Situated on a hill facing Narragansett Bay, it has a bird's-eye view of the beautiful surroundings. Known as a yachting center today, yesteryear's memory prevails throughout the entire city. Beautiful old buildings, such as the Clement Weaver House (1679), General James Mitchell Varnum House (1842), the Armory of the Kentish Guard, who claims the second greatest general next to George Washington, General Nathanael Greene, as a member, was built in 1842.

And then there's Providence, that closet of history, founded by Roger Williams in 1636 as a home for freedom of thought, word, and deed. Today Providence is the state capital, home of diversified manufacturing, and one of the largest cities in New England. Historical tours are a must, and plan to take plenty of time to see everything. Historical houses are so plentiful, both 18th- and 19th-century homes, many original, many restored. There's the Thomas Poynton Ives House, built in 1806; the Edward Carrington House, built in 1811; the magnificent home of John Brown, built in 1786, which is now home to the Rhode Island Historical Society. Meeting halls and professional buildings of historical significance are plentiful: the Old State House, 1762; the First Baptist Church, whose congregation was first formed by Roger Williams in 1639; and the Brick School House. There are outstanding museums andd libraries offering invaluable art and book collections; period pieces of American furniture, jewelry, silver, and the list goes on and on.

The city of Providence and the surrounding area cannot be hurried through. Deep within the heart of this city are stories of heroism and bravery, fear and excitement. It's a bustling, thriving city that provides a strong economic base for its residents, or a place of great opportunity, just for the asking.

Travel south from Providence through Bristol County along the eastern shore of Narragansett Bay to Barrington, Warren, and Bristol. These little towns were originally owned by the Massachusetts Bay Colony, but were released to Rhode Island Province in 1747. A quick hop over the bridge will place you on Aquidneck Island, home ground to Portsmouth and Newport.

Portsmouth, the second oldest settlement in Rhode Island, was founded by William Coddington in 1639. Anne Hutchinson and family soon followed. Hutchinson was a rebellious and banished Puritan of the Massachusetts Bay Colony who fought for freedom of religion and thought. In 1700 Quakers built a meeting hall that is still standing. Green Animals Topiary Gardens is nearby. Started in 1880 by Thomas Brayton, trees and shrubs are sculpted into animal shapes.

Opulent Newport is located on the southern portion of Aquidneck Island, the largest of some 32 bay islands. Long recognized as the resort of the wealthy, there is much to see and much to do in Newport. Those ever popular elegant mansions, built by the *very* wealthy as summer cottages, dot the eastern portion of Easton Point. There are dozens of historic homes and buildings brimming with stories of happenings and events held within and throughout the greater Newport area.

Some of the oldest buildings of worship — Touro Synagogue, built in 1763; the Friends Meeting House, dating from 1699; and the beautiful and graceful Trinity Church erected in 1698, are located here. Wonderful and exciting museums enrich the city: the Newport Art Museum and Art Association, the Naval War College Museum, the Museum of Yachting, and of course, the International Tennis Hall of Fame and Museum. The famous Redwood Library, named for Abraham Redwood, who in 1747 helped establish this prestigious library, houses priceless volumes of historic literature.

The Newport Music Festival is a must-do experience for summertime. All types of theater and musical presentations are available. Newport has such a variety of interests that boredom does not prevail.

With the completion of the 2¹/₂-mile-long Newport Bridge in 1969, travel to Conanicut Island was made easier from Newport. The island was named for

Narragansett Indian chief, Conanicus. The town of Jamestown sits on the southern portion near Fort Wetherill State Park. There's abundant history on lighthouses here, with plenty about its own Beavertail Lighthouse. Three military forts stand guard over Narragansett Bay. The Jamestown Museum can answer any and all historical inquiries. Now, cross over the Jamestown Bridge and you're back on U.S. Highway 1.

Go inland and investigate the many rivers, lakes, forests, and historical landmarks that pop up everywhere. Delve into the history of Hope Valley, that little milling village established in 1770. Travel to and through 14,000-acre Arcadia State Park, where facilities for picnicking, hiking, boating, fishing, and winter sport activities are available. There are excellent waterways and reservoirs scattered throughout the state, the larger lake area being Scituate Reservoir. Rural roads and lanes, state highways and thoroughfares, and the super Interstates will transport you through towns and villages that can expose you to Colonial, Indian, Revolutionary, Civil, and present-day history that is so intriguing that you wonder how so much could have taken place in so small an area.

Explore the Blackstone River Valley and Cumberland area in the northeast corner, near Woonsocket, one of Rhode Island's largest cities. Waterpower played a great part in the development of upper Rhode Island, both industrial and recreational.

The Blackstone River, named for William Blackstone who arrived in 1635 and settled in northern Cumberland near Lonsdale, travels across the northeast corner, entering from Massachusetts through Woonsocket toward Providence. As it picks up strength, Blackstone becomes Pawtucket River, then Seekonk river, which flows into Narragansett Bay. Water drove the waterwheels that powered the mills and factories along its route. Many of those industrial structures are still standing.

Small towns and villages simply chockfull of history, both in anecdotal and visual form, can be experienced throughout all of Rhode Island.

— Barbara J. Shangle

# Vermont

Two resources stand out over all the rest that Vermont has been blessed with since her beginning. Those are, simply said, her land and her people. You cannot overstate the terrific beauty of this land. And, too, it is quite impossible to know the people of Vermont without admiring them profoundly. While Vermonters protectively watch over their land with an iron-like tenacity, their Roman goddess, Ceres, watches over them. To know this land, you must know her people. Likewise, to know Vermonters, you must know their land. There is a certain richness in the people that will remain nondescript.

The earliest settlers — the Indians, French, English, and Yankees — of this region we now call Vermont were all independent thinkers, who fought for their freedom and their homes, and who learned to survive through extraordinary hardships. Because Vermont is a land that only rewards persistent industry, the pioneers who settled this area developed the skills in discipline needed to conquer this frontier. The legend of Ethan Allen and his Green Mountain Boys probably most accurately characterizes the people of Vermont and their stormy struggle to gain sovereignty for their state.

*Verd*, meaning "green" in French, and *mont*, meaning "mountain," Vermont derives its identity from its enchantingly beautiful green mountains. The Green Mountains are blessed with the rugged beauty of the mountain range that strikes out through the center of the state. Dotted with hundreds of snow-capped mountain peaks during the winter, and frosted with countless acres of majestic evergreen trees year round, this northern link of the Appalachian system serves up a winter playground treat that is visited by thousands every year.

Vermont's unsurpassed scenery is a pearl in the country's cache of most beloved treasures. There is never a more memorable moment than when you gaze upon hillside after hillside, all aglow with the truly spectacular red, orange, and yellow hues of the Vermont maples. Maple trees, all ablaze in autumn, are set off by a rich tapestry of evergreens. It is this gorgeous land that Vermonters have conquered, defended, and learned to love.

Most attractive to tourists and natives alike is the region's excellent ski facilities. Stowe, a small mountain village located north of the heart of the Green Mountains, is considered the ski capital of the East. This ski resort/summer vacationland owes much of its fame to the location of Vermont's highest peak, Mt. Mansfield.

Within sight of Mt. Mansfield is historic Smuggler's Notch, the site where both British and American goods were smuggled in and out of the country, duty free. Vacation resorts now occupy the Notch.

Trailing up along the New York-Vermont border are the Taconic Mountains, home of the largest natural body of water lying entirely within the state, Lake Bomoseen of Castleton. It is one of the most highly developed summer recreation areas in the state.

Fertile valleys and more than 400 lakes and ponds cut through Vermont forming an area of scenic variety unequaled in New England. Nearing some towns, the alert visitor can sometimes sight a tall steeple before crossing the last verdant meadow into one of Vermont's many historic towns.

Added to Nature's beautiful landscapes and sparkling maple trees, one first discovers Vermont's most treasured manmade landmark, the covered bridge. Every one of Vermont's 114 covered bridges has a story behind it, and each one illustrates a feeling of lasting romance among the people. There are more covered bridges here than in all of the other New England states together.

For the enthusiastic hiker who wants to absorb all of these Vermont wonderments, the Long Trail is the perfect route. Starting at the Massachusetts border, a hiker can wind north to the Canadian frontier, approximately 261 miles. Traveling south to north, the majestic vistas of New York's Adirondacks, Vermont's Lake Champlain, and New Hampshire's White Mountains are easily viewed.

The Valley of Vermont is nestled in between the Taconic Mountains on the west and the Green Mountains on the east. This long and beautiful valley, which begins at the Massachusetts-Vermont border and continues as far north as Brandon, is sprinkled with treasures awaiting an appreciative discoverer.

Starting in the south and traveling north where the valley widens into the Champlain Valley, the visitor will first discover charming and historic Bennington, headquarters for the famous Green Mountain Boys and Ethan Allen. The fascinating Bennington Museum houses the oldest Stars and Stripes in existence, the famous Bennington flag, as well as military memorabilia, colonial furniture, and a large collection of Grandma Moses paintings.

The valley's most important river, and also the longest in the state, is Otter Creek. And when mentioning rivers, Batten Kill makes itself present. Both waterways offer exceptional fishing.

Vermont has long led the nation in the production of marble, as the busy quarries at Danby and Proctor illustrate. The headquarters of the Vermont Marble Company in Proctor has been called the "center of the marble world." The state also ranks as the country's leading producer of granite.

The gentle, rolling hills and meadows of the beautiful Champlain Valley have enticed man since Samuel de Champlain and the Algonquian and Iroquois Indians first called this place their own.

The Vermont Lowlands-Lake Champlain area is situated between the Green Mountains on the east and New York's Adirondack Mountains on the west. The valley opens out toward Canada from its southern point at Brandon. Valley residents often frequent the state's largest and most beautiful city, Burlington, as well as the many other rural towns. The Valley is steeped in a history of several peoples warring over its riches.

Rich in tales of its glorious past, Champlain Valley is even more wealthy with its present resources. Burlington hosts scenic ferry trips across Lake Champlain, the nation's third largest natural freshwater lake outside the Great Lakes. St. Albans, a short drive due north from Burlington, hosts the Maple Sugar Festival every spring. Nature lovers are provided a 5,000-acre wildlife refuge at West Swanton.

Common to both Vermont's Piedmont region and the Northeast Kingdom are many scattered, beautiful lakes. This is Vermont's lake country. The Piedmont is the eastern foot of the Green Mountains. The Northeast Highlands are outlined by Essex County, which is bordered by New Hampshire and Quebec, Canada.

Lake Memphramagog is the second-largest lake in the state. Owned jointly by Vermont and Quebec, the lake's port city, Newport, known locally as the Border City, is a popular gateway between Canada and New England.

Picturesque Lake Willoughby, near Westmore, has been proclaimed the nation's most beautiful body of water. It has been compared to Lake Lucerne of Switzerland. Other important and scenic waterways include the Connecticut and Winooski rivers and Lake Averill. The Connecticut forms the entire eastern border. The beautiful Winooski River canyon, often compared with the grandeur of western river canyons, cut a deep 4,000-foot valley through the main range of the Green Mountains.

South of the wilderness area is the largest city in Vermont's northeastern sector, St. Johnsbury. This busy little community maintains three fascinating museums: The Fairbanks Museum of Natural Science and Planetarium; the Maple Grove Maple Museum; and the unique art gallery and library at the St. Johnsbury Athenaeum. A bit farther south is Vermont's state capital, Montpelier, and the busy, industrious work of neighboring Barre, where the Rock of Ages Company operates the world's largest granite quarries and granite finishing plant.

The southern counties of the Piedmont — Orange, Windsor, and Windham — are dotted with historical sites and interesting stories. Sharon is the birthplace of Joseph Smith, founder of the Mormon Church. There is industrial Harford and White River Junction, and the charming village, Norwich, which typifies a scene of Old New England. There's historic Windsor and Bellows Falls, plus Putney, home of "Santa's Land, U.S.A." The list goes on and on.

Vermont is a place where visitors and residents alike can immerse themselves deep into history and adventure. The state's rich history and lively tales of yesteryear's adventures, and its endless variety of dreamlike natural resources, make Vermont a pearl in the treasury of jewels.

— James Michael Fagan